THE HEYDAY OF THE BUS: MIDLANDS

J. B. BUCKNALL

IAN ALLAN
Publishing

Front cover:
Walsall No 310 (BDY 819), new in 1947, was acquired in
1959 from Hastings Tramways (Maidstone & District),
being a Sunbeam W with BTH electrical equipment and
Weymann H30/26R body. Maidstone No 44 was one of
eight trolleybuses, all of which had their bodywork
extensively rebuilt after arrival at Walsall, here
photographed in Carl Street, which was the rear
entrance for trolleybuses entering Birchills Depot. The
limited size destination window was too small to
display the Leamore blind fully.
Jack Haddock

Back cover, left:
Daimler Fleetline No 381 graced the Coventry city
centre on 7 October 1978, running as WMPTE No 381Y
(CRW 381C), and was the final vehicle in a batch of 21
CRG6LX buses with Willowbrook H44/32F bodies
supplied to Coventry in 1965. The Fleetline proudly
displays the classic Coventry livery while operating a
'Monobus' single crewed service to Fenside, and was
based at Sandy Lane garage (code 'S').
David J. Hughes

Back cover, top right:
The Thursday and Saturday market-day services to
Ashbourne pass through some of the most spectacular
and picturesque countryside anywhere in Britain. The
villages of Wetton, Alstonfield, Tissington, Fenny
Bentley, Thorpe and Ilam have great natural beauty and
old-world charm, typical of the valley of the Dove.
A journey on W. N. and S. M. Warrington's 1981
Bedford SB5 with David Pickering at the wheel is a
magical experience. Narrow winding roads, severe
bends, fierce gradients and scenery to stun are the result
of nature's handiwork, while the human hand has been
kind on the landscape, producing settlements of
character and great charm. The willing and hard-
worked Bedford is depicted passing over Lode Mill
bridge as it crosses the Dove, beloved river of the
legendary Isaak Walton. Occasionally the 'boss' takes a
turn at the wheel, his wife the 'bingo' run. Family
transportation indeed! *Author*

Back cover, bottom right:
A display of trolleybus flexibility! *Zöe*, JTO 313, an
immaculately kept ERF eight-wheeler with white tyres,
owned by Bloxwich based showman Pat Collins, has
stopped with a puncture while hauling the 'Super
Dodgem' ride. Overtaking a Wolverhampton trolleybus
No 445 (EJW 445), new in 1947 as part of an order for 15
Sunbeam W's with Park Royal 28/26R bodies (EJW 434-
448). All were rebodied by Roe between 1960-62, No 445
in 1962. A 6LW generator set is in the trailer.
Jack Haddock

Introduction

On being asked by Peter Waller to follow
A Celebration of Steam: West Midlands with a bus
book in the 'Heyday' series, again covering the
West Midlands, I thought that the problems
likely to be encountered would be similar — how
to get a quart into a pint pot. As with the earlier
book, there was a vast area to be covered but
with fewer illustrations. There was, however, a
bonus — this book was to be in colour. With
many huge municipal authorities operating bus
fleets and a with vast number of independents
and subsidiaries of major groups, there was an
almost infinite number of vehicle types and
livery variants to be illustrated. The liveries
encompassed both the subdued and the strident,
whilst vehicle types included single- and double-
deckers, buses and coaches and even
trolleybuses. Body styles, too, were infinite —
rear-entrance and forward-entrance, lowbridge
or highbridge. Some of the buses were successful;
others less so. But all could claim a place.

Buses were running well before the 1920s; the
free spirit and the flexibility of the bus
contrasting strongly with the tram, tied as the
latter was to its track and overhead. The
flexibility that the bus offered was exploited in
1913 by the London & North Western Railway to
provide feeder services to its stations at
Hednesford and Brownhills using buses
provided by Milnes-Daimler and Commer Cars.
The volunteer crews of the vehicles concerned
were locomotive crews based at Ryecroft depot,
Walsall, whilst the conductors were station staff
from Brownhills.

The year 1913 was certainly not the heyday of
the classic bus, but from such early beginnings
men with vision pioneered route and fleet
development; the age of the bus had dawned.
Sedentary populations could, for the first time,
venture 40 or 50 miles away and return home in a
day, going where they wanted and not where
steel rails led. New sights were witnessed and
new horizons were opened up as the internal
combustion engine applied torque and rotation
to the wheel, ever more quickly, ever more
reliably and with ever increasing power.

Gavin Booth in his *The Heyday of the Classic Bus*
thought the period of the 1950s and 1960s
represented the pinnacle of the bus. We vary in
that my 'heyday' requires a broader canvas. A
vast upheaval has occurred in recent years,
enough to challenge our perception of the

traditional bus. The motorcar has become the
primary means of private and family transport,
resulting in fewer travellers using bus services.
This in its turn results in falling revenues, a
reality that has had to be faced and which has
spawned the 'mini-' and 'midi-' revolution —
new concepts in public transport to cover new
operating conditions. Perhaps the 'heyday' of the
classic bus ran right up to this watershed of
operations, and what interpretation of 'classic'
could leave out a Reliance, Leopard, Atlantean or
Fleetline? My heyday is purely personal and
favours the period when the half-cab was in
decline, when the trolleybus was considered life-
expired and in terminal decline, and when
technologically mature buses had high capacity
with large diesel engines mounted in a variety of
locations — front, underfloor and rear.

Many of Gavin's classics still operate in rural
backwaters, cascaded to the fleets of enthusiastic
operators where they are carefully maintained
and continue to operate. The West Midlands
plays host to many of these operators. It was, in
addition, the birthplace and operational home of
many of the newer classics portrayed in this book
— most obviously in the presence of Daimler in
Coventry, Metro-Cammell in Birmingham and
Guy in Wolverhampton. I hope that you will
enjoy this selection of photographs and I would
like to take this opportunity of thanking my
friends for their expertise and vision of the world
of the bus and for their skilled camera work,
which they are able to share with you through
this book.

J. B. Bucknall, Stafford   October 1995

First published 1996

ISBN 0 7110 2444 8

All rights reserved. No part of this book may be
reproduced or transmitted in any form or by any
means, electronic or mechanical, including photo-
copying, recording or by any information storage and
retrieval system, without permission from the Publisher
in writing.

© J. B. Bucknall 1996

Published by Ian Allan Publishing

an imprint of Ian Allan Ltd, Terminal House, Station
Approach, Shepperton, Surrey TW17 8AS.

Printed by Ian Allan Printing Ltd, Coombelands House,
Addlestone, Surrey KT15 15 1HY

Title page:
To commemorate a century of public transport in Walsall, Bristol VRT No 4714 (JOV 714P), fitted with Metro-Cammell H43/33F body, was painted in the handsome South Staffordshire Tramways livery. The scheme looked back to 1885 when trams were introduced in a modest way on a few routes. Eventually, operation in the town was to pass to the local authority. Later, petrol-electric, battery and petrol buses expanded the network, although the early types proved unreliable with fairly regular recourse to the spare capacity of the Birmingham & Midland Motor Omnibus Co for assistance. Trolleybuses started to operate in the town in 1931.

No 4714 was photographed at Pye Green, near Cannock, when operating route 301 to Walsall. This vehicle has fortunately been preserved in the historic colour scheme and now resides at the Aston Tramway & Transport Museum in Birmingham, alongside many other exhibits of historical significance depicting the public transport heritage of the West Midlands area. *Author*

Above right:
Berresfords' JPA 179K was an AEC Reliance. This type was AEC's best-selling single-deck bus and by 1969 production had reached some 7,000 units. The dryliner AH505 engine or the beefier AH691 11.3 litre — which produced 157bhp at 2,000rpm in 'derated' form (205bhp for heavy road-haulage use) — was fitted. Reliance production had reached about 8,000 in 1972 when this Park Royal DP45F-bodied bus was built. It came to Berresfords in 1980 from London Country.

It was photographed at Leek bus station in a holding position prior to loading, with VDB 951 to the rear in a different livery. Berresfords was taken over in the late 1980s, to become part of the Potteries Motor Traction empire.
Clem J. Smith

Right:
Seen in operation in Burslem, Stoke-on-Trent, is Berresfords' Leyland Titan PD2 JJP 504, which was ex-Manchester Corporation. As with many operators, Berresfords was well informed about the availability of surplus stock, and the PD2's purchase was to prove a sound investment, the vehicle being in good condition and with a long life expectancy that made it well suited to Berresfords' stage-carriage needs. The body was a solidly built construction from Massey. No route or destination is displayed; a cardboard sign for Hanley in the lower cab window is the only indication of the bus's destination.
David J. Hughes

Right:
The Blue Bus Co of Rugeley, Staffordshire, commenced as a modest concern operating mini-buses, acquiring its first full-size bus in 1981. It developed alongside Key Coachways. The operation was, however, of short duration, becoming part of the Stevenson operation based at Spath, Uttoxeter.

The view depicted here, from the high edge of Cannock Chase at Flaxley, shows LAK 290G climbing through the Pear Tree Estate, with the cooling towers and emissions from Rugeley 'B' power station visible in the distance on the valley floor of the River Trent. Rugeley 'B' relied on 'merry-go-round' trains bringing in coal from the North Staffordshire coalfield or from the Nottingham/Derby area, with trains staged from Toton Yard.

Blue Bus ran a varied fleet; LAK 290G was a Leyland Atlantean PDR1/3 with H43/31F bodywork built by Met-Camm that was originally new to Bradford City Transport. Only two members of the Blue Bus fleet were taken into Stevenson ownership.
Rob Selvey

Opposite:
Birmingham Corporation transport certainly furnished many routes in the congested city centre, but outer suburban areas were also served — as illustrated by this imposing shot of No 3035 (MOF 35). This was one of 100 Guy chassis supplied to the city during 1953/54, which were bodied to traditional Birmingham style by local coachbuilders Metro-Cammell. Gardner 6LW engines were typically used. The bodywork featured the 'new front' first displayed some three years earlier on a Crossley.

The Outer Circle duty (route 11C) would provide several photographic opportunities for the cameraman during the Guy's meanderings on this off-peak service. This vehicle still exists over 40 years after its construction, being preserved and stored indoors a couple of miles from central Birmingham by Mike Wood.
Mike Wood

Above:
The variety of Birmingham buses is portrayed here in this cavalcade of the city's Guy, Daimler, Crossley and Leyland models — ideal provision for mass transportation. While the Birmingham 'standard' was the double-deck type, it is perhaps fitting that the first vehicle is JOJ 231, the first of an order for 30 Leyland PS2s built in 1950 with Metro-Weymann 34-seat single-deck bodies after the delivery of hundreds of double-deck vehicles over the years.

The same year, 1950, also brought five of Leyland's new single-deck

Olympics to the city. These were fitted with O600 engines, which were located horizontally underfloor amidships. The Transport Department was obviously cautious about the new technology, Nos 2261-2265 (JOJ 261-265) perhaps seeming a rather radical package after years of solid chassis beneath equally solid bodies with engines located at the front end.
Fred Butler

Below:
Stage services, private charter and school contract work in the Leek, Ashbourne, Winkhill and Cauldon Low area have been the preserve of the long-established Boydons operation at Winkhill for many years. Management extols the virtue of the AEC marque for quality, durability, longevity and ease of maintenance. With water, brakes, diesel and tyres supplied there are few problems.

Other vehicles are operated, but the Reliance forms the backbone of the fleet, *Bullhorns*, SIB 7882, being the family's favourite. This is a 6U3ZR fitted with Plaxton Supreme IV body. With long coaching horns at roof level, the nickname is obvious. The coach was new in 1978 and came from George, Hare Street, in 1988. The AEC was operating a school summer holiday Staffordshire Police activity scheme (SPACE) outing to Hanley recreation centre. *Author*

Above:
A jewel in present-day West Midland bus fleets is KNT 780, a legendary Leyland Royal Tiger fitted with Burlingham Seagull bodywork operated by Boultons of Cardington, Church Stretton. The superb 1954 PSU1/16 is retained in the fleet, not only as a preserved vehicle maintained to full PSV standards but also to operate on charter and, now very rarely, on occasional stage-carriage work. It can also be seen on display at rallies. This is surely the best way of preserving a 'classic' vehicle. To many aficionados, the Seagull was the most aesthetically pleasing body ever put on a coach chassis. The vehicle was recently displayed at the Great Dorset Steam Rally.

The coach was new to Dan Griffins of Crickheath, spending its first five years on Oswestry–Manchester/Liverpool services. Today the vehicle has an easier life, caringly tended and wisely operated. To see it very occasionally running through Ironbridge makes one stand in awe and admiration of the grace, elegance and subtlety of the curves and lines of Burlingham's masterpiece. *Author*

Above:
The Shrewsbury-based Sentinel company, famous for its steam tractors and waggons (which were continually upgraded and produced right up to the mid-1930s and finally culminated in the efficient S4 and S6 underfloor-type units), diversified into the internal combustion field, producing the STC4 four-cylinder underfloor-engined bus chassis post-1945. The type found limited favour, usually with minor operators in the North Midlands and Welsh border areas, although others did venture further afield.

Pictured at Donnington, near Wellington (now part of Telford), HAW 302 was a Browns example, the highly distinctive type being instantly recognisable from the front through the stylised Sentinel grille. Never prolific, the type added interest and variety to the bus scene, but never made significant inroads into the order books for major operators and never posed a serious threat to the high-volume producers elsewhere. A six-cylinder STC6 was also produced.
Graham Cox

Above:
The Ministry of Defence maintenance and storage establishment at Donnington became a focal and terminal point for bus services taking both military and civilian personnel to and from the extensive site. Britannia was another operator represented in this area, the company favouring Ford chassis. Pictured at Donnington are YHA 375J and XUX 417K, both being Ford R192s with Plaxton bodies, the former, 1971-built example was to B45F standard, whilst the latter seated two more.

While the company's operations did not feature any long-distance routes — the bulk of the work being of a local nature — the extra expense of 'heavyweight' equipment was considered inappropriate, the Fords providing a type of vehicle well-suited to the company's requirements.
Rob Selvey

Left:
Burton upon Trent Corporation entered the field of municipal transport operation in August 1905 with a limited 3ft 6in gauge tramway network, which utilised single-deck trams. The introduction of single-deck Guy buses in 1927 foreshadowed the demise of the trams (in 1929). The single-deck vehicle was dominant until 1944 when Guy-built 'Utility' double-deck buses were incorporated into the fleet. The operator's faith in Guy chassis remained for many years, with exceptions in the early years being a unique AEC Ranger 4, a Leyland Lioness and a 1945-supplied Daimler CWA6 (No 26 — FA 8009) with body built by Duple.

The photograph, taken on 4 March 1973, depicts the traditional and revised liveries used by the Corporation, with fleet No 99 being in the old maroon and white colour scheme. Behind is GFA 96D. The years from 1962 until 1964 saw a change in vehicle-acquisition policy, with batches of Daimler/Gardner 5LW double-deck vehicles being supplied with Massey H33/28R bodies.
Graham Cox

Below left:
Atlantean No 5 (205 BTP) was a Met-Camm-bodied vehicle acquired from the Portsmouth Corporation fleet, taking the number of one of the six Guy Arab III 5LW buses (Nos 2-7) supplied in 1947 with Roberts bodies. The harder riding qualities of the Guys perhaps failed to live up to the batch's registration series — FAB 595-600.
David J. Hughes

Left:
S. Butter of Child's Ercall, Shropshire, covers long-distance private charter coaching operations and local services centred on Newport, Shropshire. A considerable number of schoolchildren are carried, with several county contracts being held. All the vehicles used were built to coaching standards, the firm favouring Bedford chassis. Also operated are a Leyland Leopard, a DAF and a Leyland Royal Tiger RTC with Leyland Doyen body — a real rarity — as the main coaching fleet.

OOU 534M, a Bedford YRT with Plaxton Elite III C53F body, was purchased in 1979 from Epsom Coaches, being new in 1973. It is the most senior member of the fleet, four later YMTs commencing duties in 1977/78. As this vehicle had no operational use on the day of my visit, my thanks are expressed to the proprietor for positioning the vehicle for photography. The steel skeleton of a new large garage is being built, and should be operational when I next visit the site.
Author

Below left:
The Royal Tiger Doyen was a recent substitute hired to a local firm whose vehicle was not available. Fortunately, this gave me a unique opportunity to travel on this classic to Aberdovey. This trip also included a journey on the Talyllyn Railway. Quality exudes from this vehicle from the chassis up. The superb air-suspended ride and furnishings make this the most satisfying vehicle I have experienced. Coming home along the M54 in darkness was like coming into land without touchdown; the big 11 litre engine was hardly audible and was totally master of its job. Surely a prime candidate for preservation in due course.
Author

Above:
TCO 528 was a Cantrills bus photographed at Leamington Spa with G&G's 212 BTP, the pair showing well the use of the varying blues in the liveries of the two companies.

G&G was formerly a member of the Western Travel Group and was taken over in December 1993 by Stagecoach, which shares a facility with its associated company, Midland Red South. The photograph was taken on 10 October 1978, and demonstrates how quickly things have changed in the world of public transport. Takeovers by big nationwide companies have been common since the late 1970s, while, to help redress the balance, many small concerns have emerged to exploit niches in the market that have arisen in the post-Deregulation era. These operators often start with limited resources, with a few mini- or midi-buses, hoping to expand their enterprises as opportunities and finances allow. *David J. Hughes*

Below:

Bus services over a wide area of the West Midlands are today provided by Graham Dodd's Chase Bus Services. The fleet comprises Leyland Nationals with the exception of four Leyland Leopards. Three of these are PSU3C/2R, with No 28 being a PSU4C/2R with East Lancs body acquired from Inter Valley Link in 1989, that operation itself being taken over by National Welsh in the same year.

Starting life as a taxi business, the operator has ventured into the stage-carriage and luxury coach world steadily as the opportunity arose. The fleet now numbers some 60 buses and a dozen coaches along with a handful of mini-buses. Some of

Chase's earliest buses were several examples of ex-Midland Red Leopards, represented by No 44 (JHA 222L), which was withdrawn. The PSU3A/2R, seen at Rawnsley turning towards Cross Keys, Hednesford, was acquired by Midland Red North at its creation. It is fitted with a Marshall DP49F body and was new in 1973, being finally withdrawn from Midland Red in 1986.

Chase has adopted a Greater Manchester-style orange/brown livery, although a number of Leyland Nationals have appeared in all-over advertisements. *Author*

Above:
The Chase coaching fleet is numbered from 250 upwards. Carrying No 255, PSU 954 is a solitary Leyland Tiger TRCTL11/3R that was formerly registered KGS 488Y; a total of eight vehicles now operate with 'cherished' PSU plates. The pale blue of the coaching fleet sits well on the Leyland's Plaxton C50F Viewmaster IV body. This vehicle was acquired from Hurlock of Northfleet in 1988.

The operator's route X55, from Boney Hay to Birmingham, could be considered its showpiece. On weekdays it is the preserve of the Tiger, providing standards of comfort not usually associated with service vehicles. No 255 is pictured at Chasetown, the Junction Inn providing the background, while the modern bus shelter solidly conforms to the lych-gate entrance to land provided for recreational use of miners of the Cannock Chase Colliery Co. This company purchased the first deep-shaft mine on the Chase, first sunk in 1949, from the Marquis of Anglesey.

The Leyland reverts to coaching status at weekends and evenings as required.
Author

Left:

Midland Choice Travel, operating from
Watery Lane, Willenhall, operates a
growing fleet of Nationals. The fleet is
currently being upgraded with new
Dennis vehicles for operation on routes in
the Bloxwich, Walsall and Wolverhampton
triangle. The older of two Leopard
PSU3E/4R coaches with Plaxton Supreme
III bodies operated by the firm was built
in 1974, coming from Richardsons of
Midhurst in 1992. This view of the busy
Bloxwich High Street shows No 1
(TUB 7M) parked for a crew break whilst
awaiting its next departure, as is ex-
Hopkinson of Market Harborough No 15
(MLG 961P), a Leyland National
11351/1R/SC. Both vehicles are being
overtaken by a West Midlands
double-decker.
Author

Below left:

Whilst the choice (no pun intended) of
light green and yellow is eyecatching, the
company also has an orange and red
livery on dual purpose National No 16
(GMA 409M). This is a 1974 example and
was acquired from Ogdens of Haydock.
The bus is featured whilst waiting at its
stand for service 30 to Lower Farm about
to depart from Walsall's St Pauls bus
station.
Author

Above:

Coventry buses were no strangers to Birmingham as they had a route to Acocks Green. On route 32H, No 227 (VWK 227), one of the older ex-Coventry buses taken into West Midlands PTE stock, is seen here in immaculate condition. This Daimler CVG6 was supplied new to Coventry in 1958 and was fitted with MCCW body to H33/27R specification.

There seems to have been little care in the attempt to match the Coventry livery as the new West Midlands logo was applied. On transfer, buses with 'long-term' prospects seemed to have the new PTE livery applied first, with the new livery being based on the blue and cream of Birmingham — which operator was the largest constituent of the PTE fleet. No garage letter was carried by No 277 at this time, but 25 ex-Coventry CVG6s were drafted in to Acocks Green garage to work the Outer Circle route and a number of other services in Birmingham, bringing red buses to the streets of the city before the Coventry 'imports' were repainted. *Fred Butler*

17

Above:
Ex-Coventry Corporation No 15 (CKV 15D), running as WMPTE 15Y, brightens the city centre on route 17 duties to Fenside. The garage coding 'S' is carried, signifying its allocation to Sandy Lane depot. The bus was one of a batch of 22 (Nos 1-22) supplied in 1966, being interesting as 13 were supplied with Neepsend bodies, whilst the remainder (including No 15) had an East Lancs H44/31F equivalent. Although Coventry was initially excluded when WMPTE was first established, some three years later further boundary changes resulted in Coventry becoming part of the operation. *David J. Hughes*

Left:
In 1972 Derby Corporation received five Daimler Fleetline SRG6LX single-deck buses for one-person-operated bus and coach duties. Bodies were Willowbrook DP43F and the fleet numbers were 255-259. Two of the type, Nos 256/258 (OCH 256L and OCH 258L) are illustrated here. The batch represented Derby's first delivery of single-deck buses since 1935, with the exception of No 47 purchased in 1949.

For such a small class, badging was varied; vehicles carried Derby Corporation and Derby Borough Transport lettering and, with the acquisition of Blue Bus Services of Willington, Nos 258/259 carried badges for that operation but without the Derby crest. In addition, No 255 incorporated graphics to cover operation on the bus/rail link (service 169) on its front below the windscreen and No 257 carried a later version of the bus/rail logo.

When new, all five of the type were displayed in the Market Place for inspection by the Mayor, council members and civic dignitaries. The batch had a relatively short life, being withdrawn in 1979.
David J. Hughes

Below left:
Charles H. Roe provided the H37/28R bodies for a 1962 order for 10 Daimler CVG6 buses, Nos 135-144 (YRC 135-144). Derby had used five-cylinder buses prewar and Daimler six-cylinder engines postwar. The first 6LW-powered CVG6 joined the fleet in 1956; this engine, along with its 6LX and LXB derivatives, being used thereafter.

Standing at Derby bus station, No 138 was a seasoned veteran of 16 years when photographed on 12 October 1978. First withdrawals from the batch occurred in 1974 with the demise of Nos 139-141/144. No 136 was to soldier on into 1976, with Nos 137/138 bowing out two years later. The following year, 1979, saw the withdrawal of Nos 135/142/143, leaving No 138 as the sole survivor. This was finally withdrawn in 1980, having proved to be an excellent investment for the corporation and a justification for further orders for Daimlers.

The post-half-cab era at Derby was firmly based around the Fleetline/Roe combination, thereby continuing the strong Daimler tradition. Nos 224 (XCH 424G) and 180 (KRC 180D) represented 1969 and 1966 deliveries respectively. Frontal differences are apparent in the arrangement and spacing of the lights. Front-end treatment also differed, with the grille being replaced by a simple Daimler badge in the 1969 series.

The dominance of the Fleetline for Derby's double-deck requirements lasted for 10 years, from 1966 until 1976, although three Leyland Atlantean PDR1/1 buses (with either Weymann or Met-Camm bodies), Nos 61-63, were purchased from City of Oxford Motor Services. Fleetlines continued to be ordered until the final batch was delivered in 1980.
David J. Hughes

Below left:
In 1977 a solitary Volvo Ailsa was introduced into the fleet. No 71 (RTO 1R) carried an Alexander low-height body. The following year another 'one-off' was introduced. This was a Foden/Northern Counties double-decker, No 101 (WTO 101S). Fitted with an H43/30F body, this was one of seven chassis to be built by a partnership of Foden and Northern Counties in an effort to gain a foothold in the PSV market.

Another Volvo Ailsa, originally purchased by West Yorkshire PTE, came to Derby in 1981 as No 100. This was a B55/10 model and was fitted with an Alexander body. In 1982 two batches of upgraded B55/10 TD70s were acquired with Northern Counties H43/30F bodies (Nos 109-115 and 116-121). In 1984 Citybuses were purchased fitted with either East Lancs or Marshall bodywork.

No 118 (TCH 118X) portrays the classic and elegant Northern Counties bodywork carried by the 1982 intake. It was photographed when almost new on 24 April 1982.
David J. Hughes

Above:
The Beresford Arms Hotel, standing at the junction of King Edward Street and Station Road in Ashbourne, forms the backdrop to the Dunn-Line Leyland Atlantean MAU 616P as it leaves the market town on its run to Derby via Hulland. The East Lancs bodywork clearly stamps the vehicle as being ex-Nottingham. The firm runs several other Atlanteans, including BVT 651T, a more recent example with 47/33 seats and twin-door operation, which is also fitted with an East Lancs body.

Business seems limited on the route 109 from Ashbourne to Derby for double-deck operation. From Ashbourne the route takes the A517 towards Derby. Dunn-Line is based at Cinderhill in Nottingham. *Author*

Above:

Under local government reorganisation in 1974 East Staffordshire District Council replaced the erstwhile authority of Burton upon Trent. Prior to this date, in 1969, three 33ft-long single-deck Fleetlines with 44-seat Willowbrook bodies were placed in service, as illustrated by No 104 (MFA 704G). The new authority introduced some radical new thinking, including the Burton 'Buxi' initiative and No 104 is shown in its livery for this service outside Burton town hall on 24 March 1983. The 'sharper' image of the new livery is apparent, the red front panel proclaiming '5p FLAT RATE STOP ME ANYWHERE'. A small drop-plate at the front added 'PAY AS

YOU ENTER. PLEASE TENDER EXACT FARE'.

The concept of the 'Buxi' was to provide a cross between a bus and a taxi. As a personal 'taxi' service the big Daimler's economics must have been somewhat taxing! *Rob Selvey*

Above:
Elcock Reisen is a mixed fleet operation of high specification coaches for continental tours and extended holiday trips in Great Britain. The firm also operates stage-carriage services in the Shrewsbury, Telford, Madeley and Ironbridge area. The fleet is based around 53-seat Ford R1114s with Plaxton bodies, with mini- and midi-bus back-up for less onerous tasks.

Shropshire County Council tendered services and private contract work keeps a fleet of six Fords busy. HUJ 998V was caught leaving Telford bus station on a service to Much Wenlock via Wellington, Eaton Constantine, Cressage and Harley. This route is in reality a delightful tour, passing the Wrekin, a shapely tree-covered volcanic plug rising 1,334ft above the Shropshire plain. Impressive views are available in the rolling countryside dominated by Wenlock Edge, a Silurian limestone outcrop containing a profusion of shallow sea/lagoon fossils, including trilobites. *Author*

Above:
Ex-Midland Red No 5969 (UHA 969H) was an S23, one of a batch of 75 vehicles that represented the ultimate development of the 'S' type, which had been enlarged, improved and perfected over the years. By the late 1960s the in-house production of buses was proving uneconomic and No 5941 of this batch was the last vehicle completed by Midland Red, the remainder being built by Plaxtons of Scarborough.

The 51-seat S23s were similar to the earlier S22s, but differed in having no luggage-boot accommodation and featured windows with sliding top ventilators. For innovation, design, style and classic good looks, Midland Red bus provision over the years had unique character with few equals and certainly no superiors. The final S23 (No 5991) entered service in June 1970; after this date buses manufactured outside supplied all Midland Red's needs. No 5969 was photographed in the service of Evans of Shifnal on 2 April 1982. *Rob Selvey*

Above:
Express has extensive supported services linking Ashbourne, Wirksworth, Bakewell and Matlock, with a further area of operation taking in Heanor, Belper, Kilburn and their surrounding villages. A convinced Bristol LH/LHS user, the operator had six of the type until recently; one, SFJ114R, an LH with Plaxton Supreme 41C body, has just been sold, being replaced by a 44-seat Leyland National I (UPV 311S) acquired from London & Country.

KJD 421P is ex-Robson of Thornaby and was acquired in April 1994. Like three of the other Bristols (FBW 271W, OJD 89R and OJD 66R), it is fitted with Eastern Counties bodywork. The fifth, YVW 926, has a Plaxton Supreme F35C body. KJD 421P was photographed leaving Ashbourne on route 411 to Matlock via Wirksworth. Since this photograph was taken the bus has suffered accident damage, but the intention is that it will be repaired and returned to service.
Author

Above:
Frontline Enterprises Ltd operates an interesting fleet including, until recently, a Routemaster 5RM (formerly RM471, KVS 601). Leylands (Nationals, Leopards and Tigers) are the backbone of the fleet, with double-deck operations entrusted to Fleetlines.

YSU 953 (No 8953) is a Tiger TRCTL11/3RH fitted with Plaxton 3200E C53F bodywork. It came to Frontline, like several other members of the fleet, from Burman of Tamworth in 1992. It was photographed operating route 912 from Rugeley to Birmingham via Lichfield; the interesting architecture of Sutton Coldfield forms the backdrop, whilst the budding trees are about to burst into full leaf. *Author*

Above:
Glenstuart Travel of Four Ashes, Staffordshire, operates stage-carriage routes from Wolverhampton to Pendeford and villages further afield. The photograph depicts No 14 (WRN 14R) journeying along Patshull Avenue, Oxley (Wolverhampton). This and sister vehicle No 13 originated from Burnley & Pendle. Sold initially to Ogdens of St Helens, they passed to Glenstuart in August 1992.

No 14 was sold on 8 June 1995 to the Lancashire Bus and Coach Co and sold on. The new operator of No 14 requested No 13 also, this being recently released from Glenstuart. The 'Inseparables' once again operate new routes just a few miles from their Lancashire origin. The classy Leopard PSU4D/4R Alexander AY DP45s were new in 1977. Glenstuart operates Leyland Nationals and a single Leopard, but in a stronger red and white scheme with blue lettering. *Author*

Above:
Glovers of Ashbourne run local services to outlying villages. The company's busiest days are on Thursdays and Saturdays, when a market operates in Ashbourne. Bedford URA 481X, fitted with Duple Dominant 53-seat bodywork, awaits departure from the town's bus station on route 420 to Yeaveley. A longer route, 405, serves Clifton, Great Cubley, Boylestone, Church Broughton, Scropton and Hatton in the delightful countryside south of Ashbourne. Links to nearby villages are well co-ordinated. In this picture Glovers' Bedford stands in front of Express Motors' recently acquired Leyland National, followed by Warringtons' Bedford, whose driver David Pickering enjoys a chat (right). *Author*

Above:
Wheildon's Green Bus fleet of Uttoxeter was a small concern that more than held its own in competition against larger enterprises in central Staffordshire. Using Guys and two Foden PVD6 double-deckers (the latter with rare Samlesbury 53-seat bodies), the fleet grew steadily using Foden single-deckers. It later became more varied as Leyland Royal Tigers, AECs, Bristols, Bedfords and Seddons all appeared. The Seddons were strongly favoured in the operator's later years.

A pair of good solid heavyweights are featured here with AEC No 37 (CCP 609) partnering an ex-Crosville Bristol No 35 (VFM 596). The location is the firm's Rugeley garage. This building was adapted from an old cinema, close to the CEGB's giant 'A' and 'B' power stations in Rugeley.
Roger Kelsall

Left:
In general the unions were opposed to the single-manning of buses, a policy which was adopted to cut operational expenses in the 1960s and early 1970s when the rapid increase in private transport was already reducing passenger numbers significantly.

This Green Bus Guy Arab, with underfloor engine and front entrance, advertises at the front 'ONE MAN SERVICE, CORRECT FARE WOULD ASSIST'. Independent operators often had more co-operation than municipal concerns in the introduction of one-person operation, particularly in the smaller family-run operations like Wheildons and Harpers. *Graham Cox*

Below left:
Wheildon Seddon demonstrators included TBU 598G as a twin-door single-deck bus (No 23) and GBU 196K, which was a Seddon Inter-Urban tested with the fleet in 1973. The latter was photographed at the operator's Rugeley garage. *David J. Hughes*

Above:
Warstone's Green Bus garage is situated in Jacobs Hall Lane, Landwood, directly opposite Sutherland Farm (which the author's father used to farm). Image and cleanliness are of equal importance with customer service to this fleet and buses are kept immaculately, being washed down on arrival and also when split shifts are operated or crew changes undertaken. Only one half-cab double-deck vehicle is maintained in the fleet — No 12 (GNY 432C), a Leyland Titan PD3/3 with Massey lowbridge 33/35RD body — although this is now inactive.

The PD3 was built in 1965 and came to Green Bus from Rhymney Valley in 1981. Photographed in 1988 during a lull in activity coinciding with a crew break, the immaculate Leyland is already prepared for its next local run to Longford Estate via Ascot Drive, a round trip of perhaps three miles from Cannock bus station. *Author*

Above:

Green Bus service 4 to Penkridge via Pottal Pool is a popular route, enabling passengers from the Cannock area to visit Penkridge, a rural market town some four miles away. The attraction is an extensive covered outdoor market held on ground used on other days for agricultural and livestock auctions. The route along the A34 allows passengers to be picked up through Huntington before the pleasant run through falling countryside to Penkridge.

This Leyland Titan PD3/14, which was built in 1968/69 and fitted with an elegant East Lancs H38/32F body, was originally numbered 92 in the Stockport Corporation fleet. It passed to SELNEC PTE in 1969 as No 5892 before passing to Warstone. MJA 892G has subsequently been sold and all Warstone double-deck operations are now undertaken by Atlanteans.
Author

Above:

Green Bus has been a dedicated Leyland company over the years, although it once possessed a Guy double-decker and a rarely seen Bedford OB with Duple Vista body. This latter vehicle, which dated from 1950, came from Sargeant of Llanfaredd in 1973. The company is now a busy little operator linking Cannock with Penkridge, Wolverhampton and other central Staffordshire villages as well as operating services over Cannock Chase. The company also used to operate a Tuesdays and Saturdays only service linking Bednall with Stafford — a useful if commercially limited service for the small village.

Photographed passing Bednall House, a delightful cottage that was once the village post office, No 13 (LCB 60G) was part of a fleet that has been almost completely replaced over the last three years. The bus, driven on this occasion by George Higgins, is about to start its five-mile run to Stafford on route 473.

Author

Above:
Martin Mealey's H&M (Harvey & Mealey) Coaches did not run stage-carriage services, but was an operator that poses the question of what actually constitutes a public service. Having a range of Fords, before moving to heavyweight Leylands and Bristols, H&M was mainly a private charter, schools and holiday operator. It also provided transport for miners to collieries on Cannock Chase. Bus stops were always used for picking up and setting down and were also used to drop off children after the many school outings which the author organised as Headteacher of Oakdene

School, Chasetown.

The beautiful little Bedford OB ATS 689 was Martin's pride and joy, having been found in Scotland after a long search for such a little gem. His fleet carried *'Pride of Cannock Chase'* as its fleet name and this was at roof level on the bodywork of the Duple 29-seater. The Drumtochty destination was never altered. Following Martin's death, the beautifully restored and rebuilt vehicle once again ventured north, returning for further stage carriage work in Scotland.
Author

Above

The firm of Happy Days, formed by G. H. Austin, was an extensive coach and PSV operator for some 70 years. The operator was formerly based at Cannock and also had a garage at Woodseaves. Competition at Cannock was intense, Happy Days being situated directly opposite, and across the road from, Homers Coaches, a company that was later taken over by the Heath Hayes firm of Harpers. Happy Days withdrew from Cannock and today the garage site is occupied by a leisure and swimming pool complex. The coaching and travel company is now based at Stafford, with Midland

Red North having taken over the Woodseaves operation.

Photographed at Eccleshall, Staffordshire, on 7 April 1982, Ford R1114 No 121 (YRF 988M) picks up a passenger for Stafford. Today the company operates both single- and double-deck vehicles, mainly on contract and holiday duties. *Rob Selvey*

C. G. Harper commenced operations between Heath Hayes and Cannock with Ford Ts, Chevrolets and Star Flyers in the 1920s, using the title 'Gloria-de-Luxe'. Never referred to as a 'firm' by its employees, the concern was always known as 'the family'. A partnership was established in the 1930s between family members C. G., V., A. E., and F. Harper, not forgetting Mary Harper running the booking department. The firm grew to a unit of over 70 vehicles, taking over Homers, Reynolds, Johnson, A. P. Sanders, Dunn & Hale and A. T. Hastilow as it expanded.

Depicted here are some of the service buses at the Heath Hayes base, including No 47 (NRF 420L), a Bedford SB5 with Willowbrook body commonly referred to by the staff as the 'ice-cream cart', on the right. In the centre are Nos 50 (XRE 725) and 28 (1013E), which are both Leyland PSU1/11s with Burlingham Seagull C41C bodies. These were formerly used as front-line coaches, but were drastically rebuilt when converted into front-entrance service buses. Note the front end variation of the two Heath Hayes rebuilds; the once wide-ranging Royal Tigers had been well and truly caged. *Graham Cox*

Below left:
Harper vehicles were either acquired new or second-hand, sometimes as the result of takeovers. OLD 820 was formerly RTL1600 in the London Transport fleet. Built in 1954 and fitted with a Park Royal body, it was acquired by Harpers in July 1965 as fleet number 3. JXN 349 was an older 7RT, being built in 1948 as LT RTL26, and came to Harpers in 1958.
John Ashley

Left:
During the author's childhood, in wartime Britain, Harpers operated some venerable, but hard-working classics. Morris Dictators were used in service. A particular favourite was No 9 (TJ 2212), a 1933-built Leyland vehicle coming to Harpers in August 1935, 17 months after I was born. It remained with the operator until December 1954. The old LT5 Lion, with Leyland B34F body and constant mesh 'silent third gearbox', transported me over many hundreds of miles.

No 48 (VRF 629) was born in 1951, 18 years after 'TJ', and was a PSU1/12. It featured a Metalcraft 41-seat front-entrance body. Photographed on 21 September 1974, the Leyland had been rebodied to DP44F specification by Harpers in 1961.
Graham Cox

Below left:
No 10 (BDJ 808) was an AEC Regent III with Park Royal body built in 1951 which came to Harpers in February 1962 from St Helens Corporation. Numbered D8 by St Helens, the vehicle was rebuilt at Heath Hayes to become the operator's tow truck, operating on trade plate 361RJF.
John Ashley

Above:
M. A. and S. M. Hearsons' Knotty Bus Co of Chesterton, North Staffordshire, runs a fleet of single-deckers dominated by AEC Reliances and Swifts, typified by No 17 (JPA 171K). This 1972 Reliance 6U2R is pictured in immaculate condition at Hanley bus station. So strongly built is the type that age seems of little consequence. Maintenance is of the highest order and problems with the type are few. The takeover and ultimate demise of AEC did no one any favours and many operators, along with their drivers, wish that the AEC marque was still available. This example carries a Park Royal 49-seat front-entrance body. It was acquired from Buffalo of Flitwick in 1992. *Author*

Above:

Donnington was the location of this view of Martlews' Bedford UUJ 394 photographed on 28 October 1973.

Not being classified as a 'heavyweight', the Bedford represented a viable and cheaper alternative, although not as comfortable, to the 'big name' buses. The type did, however, prove to be tough and capable of good service and longevity with careful maintenance and care. Where traffic was lighter, both Bedford and Ford had reasonable penetration in to the PSV market, especially with the smaller concerns and those operating less remunerative rural routes.

The front-engine layout of the chassis did not allow for a front entrance. The limited size, higher revving Bedford engine gave better mpg fuel consumption than its heavyweight counterparts, but with considerably less performance. *Graham Cox*

Above:
Middleton's of Rugeley was a small concern with coaching, charter and limited stage-carriage work as its sources of income. A service was licensed from Rugeley to Birmingham and the Leopard fitted with Marshall body was ideally suited to the task, giving a quality ride into the city on what was in reality a limited-stop service. No 50 (ARN 577C) came to Rugeley from Ribble and provided valuable service in its dual-purpose role as bus and coach.

With top ventilators open, the bus was photographed on a typical summer's day, 23 June 1979. The colour scheme was almost Midland Red's, the maroon panel just below the window level being a nice feature. The vehicle was also beautifully lined out with gold. The fleet name read simply 'Middleton's'. The colour almost perfectly matches the red carried by today's Frontline fleet, the successor to Middleton's X41 Rugeley-Birmingham route. *David J. Hughes*

Above:
The Birmingham & Midland Motor Omnibus Co (Midland Red), for many years a producer of its own buses, continued the tradition with the 350-strong D7-type built between 1953 and 1957. These were lighter than the D5-type, at just over seven tons. Met-Camm used bodies with less sound-deadening materials, with the result that the D7 never matched the well-restrained noise levels of the D5, although the noise was never intrusive. Originally with seating for 58, the capacity was later increased to 63.

Typical of this successful design, No 4454 (XHA 454) was photographed in ex-works condition outside Stafford's Victoria Park whilst operating service 196 from Stafford to Birmingham via Wolverhampton. The use of body-space advertising perhaps shows the dominance of revenue over taste; the Filta-Lite adverts resting uncomfortably on the front corners mid-deck, destroying the subtle line of the body. *Author*

Above:
The 30ft-long, 8ft-wide, D9-type featured a 10.5 litre diesel engine and a front axle set back some 2ft from the traditional position. The prototype carried fleet number 4473, with the first of the production series entering service on 1 February 1960. First withdrawals occurred in 1971 and the last of the highly successful vehicles bowed out on 31 December 1979. The final group of six D9s were cascaded to Leicester Southgates, including No 5399 (BHA 399C).

The BMMO Trust preserved No 4871, with No 5399 being similarly treated by Midland Red Omnibus Co Ltd. After preservation, No 5399 was based at Cannock on loan for two years, often being used for summer Sunday Lichfield-Bridgnorth via Cannock services. It was photographed on X90 duties at Cannock bus station in 1991. *Author*

Above:

The 10.5 litre version of the KL engine was again used in BMMO's final double-deck design, the D10. This time it was coupled to a hydraulically-operated, electrically-controlled gearbox with two-pedal control. Midland Red, impressed by the high capacity vehicles of other manufacturers but not by their rear-engine concept, developed the D10-type. Introduced in 1960, it was fitted with an underfloor engine. No 4943 was a traditional 78-seat vehicle, whilst No 4944 was built with 65 seats and a second (rear) staircase and exit behind the rear axle.

Not considered a success, No 4944 (1944HA) was rebuilt to 77-seat capacity in 1962. Based in the south Midlands for the early part of their working lives, the pair moved to Stafford in 1964, remaining there until withdrawal. Both vehicles became very popular for private hire and enthusiasts' outings, as a result of the type's radical design and rarity. No 4943 was photographed at Uttoxeter on 27 August 1978.

David J. Hughes

43

Above:

The city centre of Birmingham echoed to roars of 'Albion, Albion' on Sunday 19 May 1968 when an estimated 150,000 lined the processional route from New Street station to West Bromwich to celebrate Albion's 1-0 defeat of Everton in the FA Cup Final. Midland Red services, illustrated by the D9 in the background, were disrupted as two of Don Everall's AECs take the team and civic dignitaries on their triumphal progress.

In the match, Geoff Astle's shot in the third minute of extra time rebounded from a defender and the centre forward then rocketed the ball into the top of the net past Gordon West, the Everton keeper.

Team coach CUK 523C, with police escort, is shown leaving New Street station. Visible on the right is one of the hefty and distinctive BCT bus stop signs for route 28, which served Station Street and Great Barr via Bolton Road, Small Heath and Bordesley Green East. *Mike Wood*

Left:
The series of underfloor-engined single-deck vehicles with 40-seat bodies built by Brush and Met-Camm, Nos 3000-3099, were constructed in 1946. The S6-type soon spawned improved derivatives — the longer and wider S8s being built in 1948 and the S9 in 1949. The development continued with the S14 in 1953. This type had monocoque (chassis-less) construction, rubber front and rear suspension (front independent) as well as hydraulically-operated disc brakes on all wheels.

No 5563 (AHA 163B), a type S17, typified the return to twin rear-wheeled single-deck vehicles after a flirtation with single rear wheels had proved a step too far, especially in wet or icy conditions. Photographed at Dudley in plain unlined livery, No 5563 depicts Midland Red in economy mode. A D9 with driver's door open and a D13 rear also get into the picture, as does Dudley's Silurian limestone outcropping in the distance.
Clement J. Smith

Below left:
The 75th anniversary of BMMO services was celebrated in style with No 6007 (GHA 407D) being given a superb modified livery in 1979. Cream window surrounds at both levels were complemented by cream wheels and tasteful lining out to a very high standard. Two insignia featured on the edge of the front panels mid-deck, that on the left being the National Bus Company logo — to be expected, I suppose, in 1979.
David J. Hughes

Left:
Between 1965 and 1969 Midland Red introduced 65 Leyland Leopards to the fleet — types LC7 to LC10 — fitted with a variety of bodies. The LC9 batch (Nos 5824-5838) were PSU/4Rs with 30ft 10in Plaxton Panorama bodies seating 36, later revised to 40. Stafford garage's tow truck is a converted LC9 retaining its front-end coachwork and seating for personnel employed in retrieval operations. The cut-down rear carries tools, jacks, wooden planking etc, and is well ballasted with huge concrete blocks. The old Leopard is thus still doing a fine job in this specialised role. *Author*

Below left:
Midland Red's Wellington garage perhaps goes one better, using former Harper's PD2/28 SBF 233 as its recovery vehicle. Painted in the Drawlane red, yellow and white livery, it contrasts strongly with the classic Harper colour scheme of light green and cream worn from delivery as the only PD2/28 built. In excellent condition, 'SBF' still sounds as crisp and urgent as the day it arrived at Heath Hayes with its Northern Counties H36/26D body in 1962. Now aged 33, it is proof that 'old soldiers never die'. *Author*

Above:
Midland Red North acquired five articulated buses from MAN/VW after the vehicles had spent some time on loan to South Yorkshire PTE. Nos 1801-1804 (DAK 301-304V) and 1805 (CLM 436T) had MAN/Goppel AB-53D bodies and were based at Cannock. Their main role was operation on a Cannock-Wolverhampton route. No 1804 was photographed at Rawnsley, turning outside the New Inn and heading for Prospect village and Cannock.

Big, ungainly and very thirsty, the MANs caused problems, especially on tight corners. Experience taught drivers not to mistake 'bendy-buses' as 'elastic buses', as once the articulation locked up the only remedy was separation of the two units resulting in considerable traffic chaos. Unloved since their arrival in 1984, the buses were withdrawn in 1986/87. They were subsequently exported to Australia. *Author*

Left:

Minsterley Motors' base is at Stiperstones, Minsterley, Shropshire, in an area of superb rolling countryside. All vehicles in the current fleet are carefully acquired second-hand Bedfords, with YMT, YNT, YRT and YLQ variants dominating. An exception is 510DMY, which is a Leopard PSU3E/4R with Plaxton Elite III body, which was new in 1973 and purchased from Young of Romsley in 1987.

Also visible in the yard on the occasion of this photograph was XUJ 489K with a most enigmatic destination board causing a timeless range of possibilities. *Author*

Below left:

The two YLQs in the fleet are NWK 10P and MWB 115P, which were bodied to Plaxton Supreme III specification (C45F). Both were new in 1976; 'NWK' came from Nicholls of Broad Oak in 1991 and 'MWB' was purchased from Torr, Gedling, in the same year. The former was spotted parked some distance from the garage against an ideal background to present a fine overall picture. *Author*

Left:
One of the remits of West Midlands PTE on its formation was to evaluate the provision of PSV services in its area. The heart of England, around Solihull and Meriden, seemed poorly provisioned and a private concern was able to provide a cheaper alternative than the PTE itself. Mid Warwickshire Motors was entrusted with the task and, receiving financial support from the PTE, commenced operation from 1 April 1978.

MWM had schools and private contract experience, works contracts and a stage-carriage service inherited from Shirleys of Meriden. MWM's Balsall Common base was vacated and relocated to Water Orton, although the move increased operating costs considerably.

MWM Leyland Panther PSUR1A/1R UVK 514G was photographed at Lapworth on 25 March 1982. The bus was new in 1969 and was fitted with an Alexander B44D body. *Rob Selvey*

Below left:
Mid Warwickshire Motors' AEC Merlin fleet is represented here by AML 665H, AML 634H and AML 636H pictured at the Balsall Common garage before the move to Water Orton. The 4P2R Merlins were constructed in 1969 and were fitted with Met-Camm bodies. The trio were photographed on 17 August 1978. MWM's operations were to prove temporary. *Rob Selvey*

Above:

North Birmingham Busways is an enterprising new operator using Atlanteans. The operator's depot is situated at Eastwoods, Wood Lane, Erdington. The company was formed by four ex-West Midlands Travel traffic supervision officials, and operates a Sutton Coldfield-Birmingham route, offering strong competition on price and service to the existing operators. The five ex-Blackpool buses are excellently turned out. The company adopted the Blackpool livery of green and cream albeit with slight modifications. All five buses are East Lancs bodied (H50/36F), four being built in 1978 and the fifth the following year. All arrived with North Birmingham in 1994.

Recently the fleet has been strengthened by the acquisition of ex-Plymouth Park Royal-bodied examples and by two from Southampton, which are also ex-Plymouth. Pictured is ex-Plymouth No 29 (STK 129T) which is caught starting its Birmingham-bound journey at Sutton Coldfield. *Author*

Above:

The Potteries Motor Traction Co's extensive network has a considerable influence on central and north Staffordshire, with the operator having both stage-carriage and coaching interests. PMT has operated a very interesting fleet of vehicles. No 172 (FEH 172J), a solidly-built AEC Reliance, was supplied with Alexander Y DP49F bodywork; it was a very comfortable 'semi coach'. This photograph, featuring the vehicle in PMT coach livery, was taken at the old Newcastle under Lyme bus station in 1972.

Of considerable interest in the view is the timing clock, where staff punched in arrival and departure times to ensure that management could keep a strict supervision of daily operations. Late arrivals obviously had to be explained, whilst early departures leaving customers stranded, automatically resulted in a three-day suspension without pay. The Gledhill-Brook time recorder at the loading point is now a museum piece. Similar clocking-on routines were witnessed dozens of times at Walsall Corporation's Bloxwich bus station during the author's schooldays, remembered by the accompanying 'clunk' of operation. *Clement J. Smith*

Above:

This Daimler CVD6 (900 EVT) was exhibited at the 1958 Commercial
Motor Show and was the only one of the type purchased by PMT. The bus
had an exhaust-driven turbo and carried a Northern Counties 69-seat body.
In 1964 it was fitted with a Leyland 9.8 litre O600 diesel engine. It was
withdrawn from service in 1972. It is pictured, during a quiet moment in its
life, at the Queen's Gardens, Newcastle under Lyme.

Following withdrawal by PMT it commenced an interesting second
career north of the border, going to Allander of Milngavie. In June 1973 it
joined the fleet of Rennies of Dunfermline, moving on yet again in March

1974 to Silverline of Thornbank, perhaps creating a record for an 'English'
Daimler in serving three Scottish independents.

For those interested in PMT vehicles, there is the Potteries Omnibus
Preservation Society, which was founded to preserve buses from PMT and
is now a registered charity. To date it has four buses. The restoration of two
is almost complete and they can be seen regularly at rallies around the
country. Further details can be obtained from the Membership Secretary,
c/o 2 Longley Road, Longton, Stoke-on-Trent ST3 4AT.

Clement J. Smith

Left:
The city of Stoke-on-Trent originated in six towns: Burslem, Fenton, Hanley, Longton, Stoke and Tunstall. Today Hanley dominates as the principal commercial and shopping centre, but each town has retained its individuality. Here PMT No 604 (OEH 604M), a 1974-built Bristol VRT SLG6 (one of the first batch of the type supplied to PMT) is seen in Burslem. The bus was Gardner-powered and featured a typical Eastern Counties H43/31F body.
Clement J. Smith

Below left:
Being cosmopolitan in taste, but with a keen commercial appreciation of the heavyweight PSV chassis, PMT was a solid supporter of both Leyland and AEC. With a Bedford van on its heels, Leyland Leopard PSU3/1R No 952 (952 XVT) carries its 1963 Willowbrook body in style, making its presence known by the typically robust Leyland exhaust. A big cat's roar subdues a less volatile Volvo's sound presence any day!
John Ashley

Above:

While central Staffordshire is relatively flat, except for the rolling hills of the Cannock Chase area, northern Staffordshire is decidedly hilly, the Congleton/Leek area of the Staffordshire moorlands having considerable gradients to be encountered on many of its bus routes. As a result the National Bus Company sponsored trials to determine the most suitable vehicle for operation in hilly areas.

No 700 (XBF 700S) was a 1978-built Dennis Dominator supplied with Alexander H43/31F bodywork, which later passed to Maidstone & District after PMT operation. The other vehicles evaluated were a Bristol VR with Leyland engine (No 686 [YBF 686S] which carried fleet number 600 during the trials) and one of the handful of Foden/Northern Counties combinations manufactured when Foden sought to enter the PSV market. All the vehicles were 1978 models and the Bristol was adjudged the winner. *Clement J. Smith*

Left:
Procters was a minor north Staffordshire operator with bus and coaching operations fitting into the niches left by the dominant PMT. An ex-Tayside VRT/LL3/6LXS came to the firm in 1980. This carried Alexander H49/34D bodywork and was originally new in 1976. The commercial centre of Hanley was the principal focus of the company's bus operations, the large and well-laid-out bus station being the nodal point used by several operators. The Bristol is shown climbing away from Hanley on the company's route 16 to Leek. *Rob Selvey*

Below left:
Procters' present fleet numbers over 20 vehicles, all single-deckers. The majority are Leyland Leopards and Tigers. Plaxton Supreme V Express-bodied Leopard HIL 7623 awaits departure from Leek with a return working to Hanley. The Supreme V body has less deep windows than the Supreme IV. Procters is yet another Staffordshire operator to possess a Leyland Royal Tiger RTC with rare Leyland Doyen body; this is HIL2376 which was new in 1976. *Author*

Above:

Stevensons of Spath, Uttoxeter, has garages strategically placed to cover its very extensive operating area that encompasses much of the West Midlands. The operating fleet consists of just over 300 units, for operations that include charter and touring work as well as stage-carriage duties. The influence of Stevensons has increased through astute takeovers and by the careful purchase of good quality second-hand buses.

Originally No 20 in the fleet, 5909W was a 1960 vintage Leyland Leopard with Burlingham DP41F bodywork. Acquired by Stevensons in the early 1970s, the dual-purpose Leyland was originally part of the Sheffield fleet as No 1009. It was photographed close to Stevensons' Spath headquarters. Also featured is the photographer's trusted D7 Bantam motorbike, which over the years took him many thousands of miles on bus reconnaissance trips up and down the country. The present day No 20 (784RBF) is a Volvo B10M-61 coach with Jonckheere Jubilee body, which came from Telling-Golden Miller in 1993. *John Ashley*

Above:
Stevensons No 30 was a venerable Leyland PD3/4 with Massey 68-seat lowbridge body. It was photographed at Burton upon Trent on 4 October 1986. Very few lowbridge buses are operating today; No 30 was given a life extension by being re-engined with a Leyland O600 in 1986. Very smartly turned out in the company's yellow, black and white livery, it is featured operating route 5 to New Street and Anglesey Road and certainly not giving away its 1968 building date.

The Leyland was yet another astute buy, coming from Rhymney Valley/Bedwas & Machen in 1982. A classic Leyland in a striking livery, PAX 466F was a vehicle highly suited for ultimate preservation — a fine reminder of the half-cab era.
David J. Hughes

Above:

This classic photograph of a vintage Stevensons line-up at Spath was taken on 8 April 1973. It features three Leylands and two AECs. Nearest the camera is Titan PD3/1 No 23 (3908 WE), fitted with Roe H41/32R bodywork. Parked in close rank next to it is AEC Regent V No 8 (966 CWL) with Weymann bodywork that was new to City of Oxford Motor Services in 1958 as No 966 and passed to Stevensons in 1970. In the centre is Leyland 564 FTF. The adjacent AEC appears to be 539 AJO, whilst the final member of the quintet is No 17 (3914 WE), a further Titan/Roe which came from the same batch as the Leyland nearest the camera. The alternation of Leylands and AECs was a nice touch, but whether the group was deliberately posed or randomly positioned cannot be verified. What can be said, however, is that the group typified Stevensons of Spath at its best. *Graham Cox*

This AEC Routemaster in the Stevenson fleet was photographed at Derby bus station *en route* to the National Tramway Museum at Crich with a charter. No 28 (RCN 699) had Park Royal bodywork and was delivered new to Northern General, the only operator apart from London Transport to acquire new RMs. No 28 was renumbered 52 in February 1983; renumbering was a regular exercise for the company. For example, No 55 (HNK 145G), a Leyland Leopard with Plaxton bodywork, had two rapid number changes in 1985 — firstly to No 24 (April) and then to No 105 (October) — thus carrying three different fleet numbers in the same year. Ford R1014 OEH 512P carried the following numbers during its career — 6, 15, 18 and 18A, whilst CHG 551C had four numbers — 20, 31, 31A and 51 — in the space of just over a year in 1980/81! To keep up with the complexity of the fleet's numbering, overtime with a pen and a telephone hotline to Spath are essential.
David J. Hughes

Below left:
Stevensons purchased several ex-London Transport DMs. One of them, No 34 (KUC 974P), is pictured here at Stowe keeping up the service in wintry conditions on 11 December 1981. Sister vehicle No 33 (KUC 973P) became the first bus in the fleet to carry an all-over advertisement, but No 34 seems content to carry its LT red livery in this delightful winter study.
Rob Selvey

Above:

Walsall Corporation No 342 (NDH 959) was the penultimate of 10 vehicles (Nos 334-343) ordered from Sunbeam for delivery in 1951. British Thompson-Houston electrical equipment was used, with bodywork being supplied by Brush. The first of the batch was displayed at the 1950 Commercial Motor Show. No 342 had its body removed in 1960, with the chassis being used for experimentation for possible future bus-lengthening projects.

As rebuilt, No 342 featured in last day operations over the system on 3 October 1970 — a day of thick, black, driving clouds with glimpses of the sun counted on the fingers of two hands. However, No 342 fortunately found the sun when captured in Bloxwich High Street. The trolleybuses were well patronised during the day by visiting and local enthusiasts. Following Walsall's closure, only two systems — Teesside and Bradford — soldiered on. The former closed in 1971 leaving Bradford as the final operator, the last trolleybuses operating in that city on 26 March 1972.
Author

Above:
Also active on the last day at Bloxwich was No 875 (GFU 693), which was a
BUT 9611T with Metro-Vick electrical equipment and Northern Counties
H39/30F bodywork. This vehicle came from Grimsby-Cleethorpes in 1962
and, like Nos 874/876/877, was originally new in 1950. No 874 entered
service in Walsall with its original body, but Nos 875/877 were rebuilt and
lengthened, being converted to front-entrance operation.
  Also purchased second-hand in 1962 were Nos 344-347 (ADX 193-196)

and Nos 351/352 (ADX 189/190), which were all Sunbeam F4s with BTH
equipment that had been delivered new to Ipswich. With little call for new
trolleybuses in the country, the acquisition of spares became increasingly
difficult; perhaps this was one of the principal reasons that many operators
abandoned the trolleybus. As a result, bargains were to be picked up and
Walsall gratefully received a number of vehicles from other municipal
operators, many of which were in a good and serviceable condition. *Author*

The development of Walsall centre and the dominating Townend Bank high-rise shopping complex resulted in intense problems for the Transport Department during the period of construction. This illustration shows clearly the difficulty of running an intensive and tightly intervalled service at this time.

Featured on the right is No 860 (TDH 910) which was supplied new in 1955 as one of 15 large two-axle Sunbeam F4As with BTH equipment and Willowbrook H36/34R bodies. These were the first 30ft-long 8ft-wide trolleybuses allowed; Walsall got special dispensation for two-axle operation from the Ministry of Transport. The extra size and capacity of the Willowbrook bodies certainly helped alleviate the rush-hour problems in the town and surrounding densely populated areas.

Also featured in this view is No 875 (GFU 693) again. Built in the same year, 1950, was No 351 (ADX 189), a Sunbeam S4 delivered new to Ipswich. The latter carried a Park Royal H30/26R body. Numbered 119 in Suffolk, it came to Walsall in 1962. *Jack Haddock*

Below left:
No 350 (RDH 990) was supplied to Walsall as a 30ft-long, 8ft-wide, three-axle trolleybus in 1953; its original fleet number was 850. The large Sunbeam S7 with Willowbrook body was laid out for PAYE operation, having a conductor's desk and standing accommodation for 15. Nicknamed 'Cox's Folly', after the then General Manager R. Edgeley Cox, the succeeding 851-865 series was introduced two years later to the same dimensions but on only two axles. After trial running, No 850 was rebuilt to H36/27R layout in February 1961. No 350 is portrayed in Coalpool Lane, north Walsall.
Jack Haddock

Above:

Relaxation of Ministry of Transport rules to legalise 8ft-wide PSVs enabled Walsall to purchase five Leyland PSU1 buses with Leyland bodies in 1952. Numbered 801-805 (PDH 801-805), these were followed one year later by five more PSU1s, this time with Park Royal 42-seat bodies. No 808 (PDH 808) of the second batch was revised to DP40F specification with more luxurious seating for dual-purpose bus/coach operations in August 1959. No 810 (PDH 810) was similarly treated in 1961; it was easily

recognised by the fact that its livery was reversed to cream with a blue stripe. The remainder of the second batch, Nos 806/807/809, were converted to one-person-operation in December 1961.

No 804 of the first series is featured in this night-time fairyland portrait; the Birchills depot's outside lighting modifying the colour of the 6in fall of snow to a pastel orange. Cosseted inside the depot was a group of Willowbrook-bodied two-axle trolleybuses. *Jack Haddock*

Left:

Lined up at Walsall, three double-deck vehicles pose in the St Pauls offices' car park. The vehicles concerned are Nos 10, 65 and 822. Guy Arab III No 10 (MDH 306) was one of 15 vehicles supplied new in 1948 with Gardner 5LW engines. A further 25 of these stylish buses were delivered the following year. An additional 10 in 1950 made a class of 50 Arabs (MDH 301-350) in service. The fleet numbers of the first batch tended to be random.

The Park Royal bodies contrasted strongly with the angular body of 'austerity' No 65. This Guy Arab II was supplied with Strachans body constructed to wartime specification, being fitted with slatted wooden seats when delivered in 1944. No 65 became No 165 in March 1963, being withdrawn and sold to Bell of Hagonfield later the same year.

The trio is completed by No 822 (TDH 769), a more modern and comfortable AEC Regent V fitted with Park Royal H33/28R body.
Jack Haddock

Left below:

Following the absorption of Walsall Corporation into the new West Midlands PTE, trolleybus operation was quickly eliminated, leaving a huge void in operational capacity. The gap was temporarily plugged by drafting in elderly half-cab double-deckers from West Bromwich and Birmingham until new buses were delivered. To locals it seemed as though the town had been invaded by buses from another planet. This striking picture, taken from the top of the St Paul's Street car park, shows the influx of 'new' vehicles. Walsall's immense range of chassis and body types in seemingly endless combination became ever more complex.

It was obvious that the new super authority, with its potentially vast fleet, would need to standardise hundreds of vehicles from only a few types in the interests of commonality of spare parts, maintenance and commercial operation.
Jack Haddock

Above:

In 1954 Walsall received four vehicles for performance and economy comparison. Photographed on route 5 in Lichfield Road, Walsall, is Leyland PD2/14 No 823 (TDH 770) equipped with a lightweight MCCW H32/28R body. The other vehicles acquired for the tests were No 400 (TDH 99), a 7ft 6in-wide Daimler CLG5 with NCME H32/28R body; No 821 (TDH 673), a larger 8ft-wide CLG5, again bodied with Northern Counties but with an additional five seats on the upper deck; and finally No 822 (TDH 769), a classy AEC Regent V with Park Royal H33/28R body. Living near Stafford, the author was used to D9s on the 865/65 route from Stafford to Dudley, a route which also used Walsall buses on the hourly service. Standard Walsall provision for this route were Roe-bodied PD2/12s delivered in 1953, which were superb vehicles and the equal of the D9s.

The four competitors appeared on route 65; No 400 was aesthetically displeasing and rode in the same mode. By this date its Gardner 5LW engine was outmoded for modern operations (90bhp at 1,700rpm). The PD2 and the Regent V were 'state of the art' chassis, riding excellently. The test results were probably futile as 1955 saw further trials with three demonstrators: a PD2/12 with experimental epicyclic gearbox; a Daimler CVG6; and No 800, a PDR1/Saunders Roe powered by a supercharged 'Comet' engine. You can't get a quart out of a pint pot, but Walsall tried.

Jack Haddock

Above:

In 1956 a single AEC Bridgemaster with Crossley body and two Daimler CVG6s with Willowbrook bodies were delivered. To add yet more variety, lightweight Bedford SBO single-deckers with Willowbrook B39F bodies followed, whilst No 400 had an equally unappreciated CLG5 partner in No 401 (TDH 401), with a body jointly produced by Metal Sections Ltd and Walsall Corporation.

In 1959 a Dennis Loline (No 800) and two PD1As (Nos 198/199, ex-Warrington Corporation Nos 100/101 and new in 1947) were added to the fleet, along with five ex-London Transport 7RTs (RTL550, 1470, 1487, 1492 and 1494). The following year brought a reversion to the Dennis fold with

16 Dennis Lolines (Nos 842-849, 878-885), all of which were fitted with Willowbrook bodies. It was not until 1961 that 10 AEC Regent Vs joined the fleet as 891-900 (891-900MDH); the first five were bodied by MCCW and the remainder by Willowbrook. It had taken some time for AEC's quality, performance and longevity to penetrate following the 1954 trials.

One of these AECs, No 896, was photographed in Lichfield Road in almost new condition; the darker paint mid-decks indicates an advertisement panel.

Jack Haddock

Above:

In 1946 Guy Motors introduced the Vixen for passenger work. The 14ft 6in-long chassis could accommodate up to 29 passengers. Butters of Child's Ercall ran 12 Vixens, all bodied by Barnard of Longwell Green and Ormac. In the 1950s London Transport ordered 84 of the type, which became the GS class, to replace Leyland Cubs on country services, wisely choosing the Perkins P6 power unit for economy. The bodies were 26-seaters constructed by Eastern Counties.

A replacement programme involving AEC Regal IVs brought the LT Guys on to the second-hand market and two were purchased by West Bromwich Corporation in 1961. MXX 341 (GS41) went to the Transport Department as No 233, whilst MXX 340 (GS40) went to the Health Department as No 49. The latter became No 252 on transfer to the Transport Department in 1963.

Both Vixens were taken into WMPTE stock, with MXX 340 being transferred to Wolverhampton and withdrawn from there in May 1973. It was subsequently sold for preservation. *John Ashley*

Above:

West Bromwich Daimler CVG6s PEA 195 and SEA 205 were acquired new in 1957 by the corporation, as part of the batch numbered 187-210. Nos 187-198 (PEA 187-198) had Willowbrook H34/26R bodies, whilst Nos 199-210 (SEA 199-210) had MCCW H37/26R bodies.

The corporation's first five-cylinder Gardner engine was purchased as early as 1934; the six-cylinder version first appeared in 1937 when No 64 was acquired for comparative tests to find the best replacement for trams in 1939. No 64 (EA 9001) was a MCCW-bodied COG6; also tested were No 63

(EA 590, a Daimler COG5) and No 65 (a Leyland TD5C). The COG6 was chosen as the victor and a batch, Nos 71-101, of the type was delivered in 1939 as tram replacements. Wartime supply limitations saw vehicles hired, loaned or acquired, with new Daimlers being delivered in 1943 (CWG5s) and 1944 (CWA6s).

Daimler also supplied CWA6s in 1945, with CWD6s following in 1947 and 1948. From 1949 onwards CVG6s were standardised, except for five CVG5s delivered in 1952. *Graham Cox*

Above:
Daimler CVG6-30s Nos 259-265 were supplied with Met-Camm bodies in 1965. Following this delivery West Bromwich continued to support Daimler by purchasing Fleetlines. CRG6LXs Nos 101-114 were delivered with H42/31F bodies in 1967/68. Photographed as WMPTE, No 107H (KEA 107E) shows a recent change to OPO status with 'Please Pay on Entry' signs prominent in three places. In the background is evidence of the reconstruction that was to lead to the demolition of so many old buildings at this time.

A further seven Fleetlines were ordered for 1969 delivery, materialising as Nos 115-121 (TEA 115-121G), but these were fitted with Eastern Coachworks H45/28F bodies. *John Ashley*

Above:

In 1957 Foden had produced a design for a rear engined (Gardner 6LXB) bus, and collaborated with Wigan bodybuilder Northern Counties to produce a new Foden NCs with H43/33F bodies. No 6300 was purchased by West Midlands, entering service in August 1977 at Liverpool Street. Almost all if its active life was on route 50, Birmingham High Street to Maypole, and also route 50N, the night equivalent. Foden made no inroad into the commercial vehicle market with the type, ROC 300R being a solitary rarity, here depicted at Digbeth on 19 October 1981.
Rob Selvey

70

Above:

Williamsons Motorways has a long history of providing transport in Shrewsbury, offering both tour and stage-carriage services to this important market town, serving Shropshire and the Welsh border country. It is fitting that 'Park and Ride' facilities are entrusted to the firm, with specially liveried Dennis Darts provided.

The fleet also contains traditional heavyweights, but the range of vehicles extends from 16 to 61 seats. UBW 788 is a Leyland PSU5C/4R with Plaxton Supreme C53F bodywork that was new in 1981 and

acquired from Hown of Barnoldswick in 1993. The Leopard is shown near the famous iron bridge in the town of that name on service X96 to Shrewsbury via Telford. Ironbridge traffic is the preserve of several local bus fleets, giving a fair variety of bus types and liveries in the town. As the cradle of the Industrial Revolution, the town, built close to the magnificent River Severn, has considerable coach traffic offering further interest and photographic possibilities. *Author*

Above:

Wolverhampton Corporation ordered eight Sunbeam F4s (Nos 623-630) with bodies by Park Royal (H28/26R) for delivery in 1950. The same year also saw the delivery of 10 Guy BT trolleybuses (Nos 645-654) with similar bodies. This represented even-handed support for both of the local manufacturers. Guy-built No 652 (FJW 652) is depicted on Pinfold Street, Darlaston, whilst operating on route 7 to Whitmore Reans. Its temporary partner is a classic Midland Red Leyland LD8 (SHA 378) on route 277, the pair making a harmonious, complementary, but contrasting comparison of typical Black Country liveries that were

familiar for many years and are now sadly missed.

A total of 100 Leyland PD2/20 buses (SHA 378-477) were ordered by BMMO. These were fitted with stylish Leyland-built 8ft-wide H30/26R bodies that tapered to 7ft 6in at the front. The bodies also had a concealed radiator grille of 10 vertical bars as specified by Midland Red. The prototype was exhibited at the 1952 Commercial Motor Show and all 100 units were in service by the end of 1953. The power unit was the solid, gutsy and understressed O600 producing 125bhp at 1,800rpm.
Jack Haddock

Above:
Seen pausing at the Pinfold Street, Darlaston, terminus, No 454 was a slightly older (new 1948) trolleybus, confirming Wolverhampton's penchant for Sunbeams. EJW 454 was a Sunbeam W with a Park Royal H28/26R body. It was the penultimate vehicle in an order for seven trolleybuses (Nos 449-455) that were the last narrow (7ft 6in) vehicles acquired by the corporation. An additional 26 Sunbeam F4s were purchased the same year to the 8ft specification. These were Nos 456-481 (FJW 456-481).

After some 12 years of heavy service Nos 449-455 received new Roe H32/26R bodies between 1960 and 1962; No 454 received its new body in 1960. Note the extreme road camber near to the gutters; this was an ever-present problem in earlier years when 'tilt' in confined streets could cause conflict with traction columns and street furniture set near to the kerb. On a journey from Stafford to Uttoxeter on board a Wheildon's Guy, the author experienced a rearrangement of a lamp-post due to the excessive camber and upper-deck roll. *Jack Haddock*

Above:
Sunbeam W No 411 (DJW 941) was supplied to Wolverhampton in 1945 with Park Royal H30/26R body and was rebodied by the same concern in 1952. No 433, its younger partner in this photograph, was registered as DUK 833 in 1946, again with Park Royal bodywork. The original bodies were removed by Guy Motors during 1958/59 and the chassis were sent to Roe for rebodying.

The location is the Townend Bank terminus at Walsall; passengers embarked for route 29 to Wolverhampton at the rear of the Savoy cinema, whilst route 1 to Hednesford and Cannock loaded at the cinema's side. The cinema has only recently been demolished, leaving an empty space void of public entertainment in a street that lost its trolleybus overhead long ago.

I remember awaiting a Walsall Dennis to Landywood in 1945 and seeing a Bassett-Lowke 'Royal Scot' for sale at £40 in the cinema's window. In those days £40 represented several years' pocket money; I gazed in awe daily. *Jack Haddock*

Above:

Having been an almost solid Gardner customer since 1942 for its new bus deliveries, 1957 was a year of decision for Wolverhampton when it decided to try locally produced Meadows 6DC engines. The rationale for this was perhaps to try and keep Gardner on its toes pricewise. Meadows were asked to power two batches of six Guy Arab IVs, while Gardner was only given the order for a single batch of six. All 18 were bodied by Metro-Camm with H37/27R bodies. No 3 (SUK 3) was one of the Meadows-powered units. While possessing the 'get up and go', the Meadows engine seems not to have possessed the Gardner engine's rugged dependability and two — Nos 6 and 2 — were re-engined with 6LWs in February 1962 and 1963 respectively.

The day of the traditional open rear platform 27ft-long bus was almost at an end in Wolverhampton, for the next order — a single bus, No 19 (WUK19) — placed in 1958 was fitted with a front-entrance Burlingham body. It was Wolverhampton's first 30ft-long bus and also boasted four-speed epicyclic gearbox and Westinghouse brakes. The bus was exhibited at the 1958 Commercial Motor Show. *Graham Cox*

75

Above:
Wolverhampton's orders for 1959 comprised two Morris 'J2' vans with accommodation for 12, while 1960 confirmed the 'new era' with the introduction of 20 Guy Arab IVs that were 30ft long and powered by Gardner 6LW engines. These were fitted with MCCW FH41/31FD bodies. No 27 (YDA 27) poses impressively outside the Wolverhampton depot, although now painted into the livery of WMPTE. Deep blue and cream buses in the depot confirm the new corporate PTE scheme and the resultant demise of the green and yellow livery of Wolverhampton that

had been so notable a part of the public transport scene in the Midlands over many years. The full-fronted No 27 and its 19 partners were to cohabit the Park Lane garage with a 1964 build of half-cab Guy Arab Vs — a strange reversion to a former standard when ultra-modern Guy Wulfrunians were the latest thoughts and aspirations for future prosperity and success for Guy Motors of Wolverhampton. Despite the hopes, however, the Wulfrunian was not a success; few were built and sold, and the type was regarded as awkward, unpopular and unreliable.
John Ashley

Left:
Running under West Midlands PTE management, ex-Walsall Corporation No 118 (now No 118L) is shown leaving Walsall St Pauls bus station in its new livery. Walsall's first 'shorty' Daimler CRG6 — a type that aesthetes may also regard as being short of good looks and not just length — appeared in 1963, No 1 being exhibited at the 1962 Commercial Motor Show. Nos 3-24 were added to the fleet in 1964, whilst Nos 25-27 appeared in December of that year.

Further Fleetline CRG6s were delivered in 1966/67; the following year's order specified the more potent Gardner 6LX. No 118 appeared as one of the batch Nos 106-119 (XDH 506G-519G) which were delivered in 1969. These received Northern Counties H41/29D bodies. By now the wrap-around windows of the earlier CRG6s had gone; the body design was more traditionally angular and the aesthetics of the front-end design were marred by a deeply V-fronted windscreen. *David J. Hughes*

Below left:
The years 1978/79 saw the delivery from Leyland of five new Titans, Nos 7001-5 (WDH 1T-5T), with bodies by Park Royal. With the PTE deciding upon at least two suppliers, it was proposed by its officers that 80 Metrobuses and 80 Titans be submitted. PTE representatives thought that a less complex and cheaper bus ought to be tried, so orders were amended to 75 each for Leyland and MCW, with 10 Dennis Dominators also ordered against the officers' wishes. Additional orders for 1979 were for 100 Metrobuses and 60 Titans. The price for the Dennis Dominators could not be held and this order was cancelled.

The Titans were to be assembled at Park Royal. However, the closure of the Park Royal works came as a blow to the PTE as it meant that Leyland was unable to fulfil its order. The result was that the order for Metrobuses was increased by 100 and the Titan order cancelled; 35 Leyland National 2s were also bought to make up the deficit. As a future 'standard' type the five Titans were allocated in numerical order to Washwood Heath, Selly Oak, Walsall, Perry Bar and Harnall Lane (Coventry). Walsall's No 7003 seen here was, like the others, centred on Perry Bar after the cancellation of the Leyland order. *John Ashley*

Above:
Worthen Travel, run by Dave Pye, continues the tradition of the name which stretches back to the 1920s. The company's principal stage-carriage service links Shrewsbury with Montgomery. URN 216R, a Leopard PSU5A/4R with a Duple Dominant body that was new to Brookfield of Stockport in 1976 and which came to Worthen in 1992, is seen taking a right turn from the B4386 to the A490 at the picturesque village of Chirbury, having passed over the remains of Offa's Dyke some two miles out of

Montgomery.

The fleet consists of three Leopards, a Bedford YRT and a Bristol RESL6G. This last-named is nicknamed the 'snowplough' as it is reputed to be the only bus to conquer the mountains in harsh borderland wintry conditions. The fleet also contains more modern DAFs and a Bova for use on coaching duties. The company also owns the beautiful AEC/Duple Britannia MVS514. *Author*

To conclude this portrait of historic buses and coaches from the Midlands, we have a montage of classic Worthen buses that were operated in past years. KUP 949 was a venerable 1949 Leyland Tiger bodied by Burlingham and is seen on a service in Montgomery. Bedford OB/Duple MHU52 was sold on to a new owner at Grange-over-Sands and is now gracing the southwest being based in Devon. Finally, the firm's MVS514, an AEC/Duple Britannia, completes this trio. This vehicle has now been preserved to show standards by the company and is the only one of the trio still with Worthen.
Courtesy Worthen Motors

The 'Heyday' series from IAN ALLAN Publishing